The Lost is FOUND

Miss Exotica

AuthorHouse™
1663 Liberty Drive
Bloomington, IN 47403
www.authorhouse.com
Phone: 833-262-8899

Because of the dynamic nature of the Internet, any web addresses or links contained in
this book may have changed since publication and may no longer be valid. The views
expressed in this work are solely those of the author and do not necessarily reflect the
views of the publisher, and the publisher hereby disclaims any responsibility for them.

Any people depicted in stock imagery provided by Getty Images are models,
and such images are being used for illustrative purposes only.
Certain stock imagery © Getty Images.

This book is printed on acid-free paper.

ISBN: 978-1-6655-1518-4 (sc)
ISBN: 978-1-6655-1517-7 (e)

Library of Congress Control Number: 2021901741

Print information available on the last page.

Published by AuthorHouse 03/11/2021

authorHOUSE®

The
lost
is
Found

CONTENTS

Chapter 1

Born to be successful

I am Miss Exotica. I came from a very poor family but I always felt in my heart I was born to be successful. I never really had the chance to prove this to myself. Having the chance to attend college would be perfect opportunity to prove to myself anything is possible if you put your mind to it. I want to become what others expected me not to become, and achieve what others have failed to accomplished.

When I was in elementary school, the kids would bully my sister Alexa and I. they made fun of us because we would wear the same hand me down clothes every day and we would switch clothes the other had on from the day before. I never really did well in school either. I never understood how some kids were so smart and I wasn't. I use to wonder how these kids knew so much. Then I came to realize it wasn't my fault. I wasn't getting the help I needed at home.

My mother Raine was a single mother raising four kids. When my mother would work I would have to stay home from school to watch my little sitter and my baby brothers. I was cooking and cleaning from the age of six years old. When my mother was unable to pay the rent we would move from house to house and school to school. Sometimes we would stay months out of school until my mother found a stable place for us to stay. School was never really important to me until I moved from Miami to Boston.

When I moved to Boston lived with my aunt Tina, her daughter Kayla and her husband Clifford. We would attend church on Sundays and Kayla and I would attend youth groups on Friday nights. I even got baptized and gave my life to Christ.

Everyone in my household was motivated and everything was about school, school and school. I attended a catholic middle school and my aunt thought it would be a good idea for me to repeat the 6th grade, so I could catch up with the other students. My first year at school was very hard for me. I hated reading aloud because I was nervous about not knowing how to pronounce a word. I hated math because I didn't know how to do it and I took longer than the other students to learn. Then I realize I couldn't be like this forever. I turned to God and I started praying.

My aunt started helping me with my school work and every day she would check my homework to make sure I was doing what I was supposed to. My aunt got me involved in after school programs that helped me so much in reading and writing better. I started making B's C's and D's in the 6th and 7th grade, but to me those grades were like A's and B's compared to all the F's I had gotten in Florida. I started feeling more comfortable and really confident. So I would ask questions and speaking my mind more.

By the time 8th grade came along, I was already determine to make the Honor Roll all year-something I had not seen myself doing. I was ready to graduate and during the summer I was already preparing myself to stay focus. I broke up with my boyfriend because I knew he was a big distraction and I put all my friends to the side. I was so anxious to start the 8th grade that this feeling in my body was ready for the challenge I was about to take on. There were times I felt like giving up or there was no hope, but the encouragement of my family helped me make it through.

I graduated from middle school on the Honor Roll and I was very proud of myself. The feeling that was inside of me that day was wonderful. Knowing that all my hard work had paid off and now I was walking down the aisle with my head held high, to receive my diploma was the best. I was even more proud to see my family right there cheering me on. Never did I ever think I would have seen that day.

Chapter 2

Memories are forever

My first few years of high school were difficult for me fitting in. I was still trying to find my identity and I was very friendly and shy. I became a cheerleader for my school and I loved singing, dancing, acting and modeling. I would wear makeup, big hoop earrings and tight clothing. All the boys in school liked me. I loved hanging out with the boys because they were always nice and kind to me, while the girls were always mean to me. They would call me names and they even tried jumping me at times. But later on in the year I made friends with four other unpopular girls and we call ourselves the grizzles. One of the girls name Sasha was managing me on my modeling career, but later quit so she could pursue her own career.

I dated one guy in high school name Jesse. He was three years older than me, brown skin, bad boy type, popular, leader of his group and all the girls liked him. He made me feel alive-true love like no other. Jesse would always make me feel safe and he even stopped those bullies from messing with me. But a year later Jesse and I broke up.

I started a new school my senior year of high school and the people were much more kind to me I learned how to defend myself and I even became co-captain of the step team my home girl Chocolate started she was also from Florida and cousin to Sasha. We had our senior class lit-Miami style. But I was still determined to graduate so I could have the opportunity to attend college for nursing school-Even though I had always wanted to be a professional dancer/actress. But my mother insisted becoming a nurse was guaranteed success and dancing and acting wasn't. My aunt also agreed and said a dance degree is limited.

I had done all my college research, applications, FASA, and my wavers for all my college choices. But two months before I was set to graduate, my aunt told me she couldn't afford to send both me and Kayla to college. So I wasn't going to ask her to choose me, nor did I expect her to send me to college and not her own daughter.

That June I went on to graduate with class of 07 with honors and I scored high on all my MCAS testing to graduate. But on a day that was supposed to be the best day of my life and celebration, in the back of my mind I felt disappointed and confused. Here was this roadblock in my path where do I go and what do I do? Something I waited and worked so hard for, the door had just slammed in my face and stopped me right in my tracks.

Chapter 3

Fast-life

One early afternoon in spring chocolate and I was downtown shopping, when we notice these two big signs that read Lady Luck Gentlemen club and Lucky Star gentlemen club. We both looked at each other and got really excited. Couple weeks earlier we had been talking about needing extra cash because we had no jobs, still in high school and living at home with our families.

Outside of Lady Luck was one of their bouncers name Jake. He was smoking a cigarette dressed in all black. Jake were this fine Irish and Brazilian gangster type guy and I immediately felt an attraction to him. I went on to ask him if we could get a tour and how do we go about getting a job. He told us we had to be at least 18 with ID and audition on Tuesday night. Chocolate and I was so excited that we started practicing dance moves. By the time Tuesday night came along we were so ready and nervous at the same time.

Chocolate and I walked into lady Luck and it was very nice inside. The lights were dim, the D.J. was playing loud country music, upstairs downstairs, kitchen to cook meals and a bar with whatever drinks you wanted. We felt a little out of place because the girls were tall beautiful thin Caucasian women and we were thick brown skin women from Florida. But we didn't let that kill our vibe.

The D.J. called Chocolate to the stage first and the stage was huge with this tall pole way up to the ceiling we were armatures so we knew nothing about exotic dancing. We both wore our under clothes with regular shoes on. Chocolate was doing the robot dance and the crowd was cheering her on. It was the funniest thing to see. Then it was my turn. My heart was racing so fast and I saw so many people staring at me. I started modeling walking and I booty shake the whole five minutes to country music. I never touched that pole once! I remembered taking a glimpse at the crowd and they were cheering me on even the women.

Chocolate had won 3rd place plus whatever tips she made on stage and I made $150.00 in five minutes. I was so intrigued and I remember feeling this rush inside of me. Later that night I called Alexa and told her all about my adventure.

The next day chocolate and I went into lucky Star and as soon as we walked inside we notice it was a much smaller middle class club. The lights were dim; the D.J was playing hip Hop & R&B music, upstairs down stairs, and a behind the bar, was this very small stage with a regular size pole. The manager John took us upstairs and showed us this woman on the camera doing these amazing pole tricks name peaches. She was slim-thick from Cape Verde. John then asked us if we could do those tricks and we both said NO! He hired me and told Chocolate she was too young.

Peaches and I became friends and she would always show me how things worked around the club. Peaches also had a pimp so she was always about making money. But as I started to find my own style, peaches stop liking me because her costumers would leave her for me.

One afternoon while I was getting ready at work a lady name Duchess ask me about my Dominican bracelet I had on. We started talking about our families and found out we were cousins. Later on I met her younger sister Candy and we became close. Candy was very short, slim-thick and she could dance her butt off. We would travel to different clubs to work until I got robbed on night after work. I was sitting in a cab waiting for Candy when this car pulled up next to us. Four guys from the club got out of the car and surrounded the cab with guns. They told me to give them my money and I could see Candy peeking outside the store. The cab driver told me not to give them my money but when I saw how this man was willing to risk his life for me—a stranger, I quickly handed over the money.

Jake and I started hanging out and we were like Bonnie&Clyde. After I graduated we got engaged and moved in together. We was living this fast life and making so much money. What an average person made in a week I made in a night. I would buy my sister and little brothers clothes, shoes, video games and whenever their lights or water would cut off I would pay it. Whenever there was no food in the house or if they needed money, I was able to send it. But I was also a saver as well. After Jake and I would pay the bills I would take only seven dollars a day for lunch and put the rest of the money away.

Jake introduced me to this drug called ecstasy. It made me feel so happy- like I was on top of the world. I remember I would talk all night and I would hug everyone even if I didn't know you. But when Jake and I did party we would dance all night-popping bottles and all eyes would be on us.

I enrolled back into school that following winter, after I found out I could use my mother's tax papers to have my school paid for. My mother was on government assistants and the government would have paid for my college tuition. This is what my mother had told my aunt to do my senior year so I could attend college but she did not.

I had gotten use to making fast money that I started to feel like I didn't need college. What a nurse was making in a year, so was I. I felt like if god wanted me to go to college he would not have allowed my aunt to stop me so I dropped out of college and I continued dancing.

All the customers at worked loved me and they made me feel welcomed. They accepted me for who I was and I wasn't being judged for how big my butt is, how big my earrings are, or what clothing I had on. I even got to dance the way that I loved and no one made fun of me. But being in this industry does have its cons as well. I would see girls strung out on drugs shootings in the club prostitution and most of these men would be married.

After a year of Jake and I dating, our relationship became toxic. We started doing more drugs and we would constantly fight over his infidelities. There were many times I wanted to go back home but I was too ashamed. My mother had disapproved of us moving in together and I was still disappointed about not getting the chance to attend college back in high school. After many times of the police being called on us for fighting, one particular night when the police was called, Jake had more bruises on him than me as well as being a smooth talker, the police arrested me and not him.

Chapter 4

the Encounter

For the first time in my life here I was with handcuffs on me, in the back of a police patty wagon and being charged with assault and battery, getting transported to jail. Never in my life did I think this would be me.my whole life flashed before me. When we arrived at the jail one of the correction officer's (C.O.) made me take out my freshly done weave, stripped me of my clothing, made me lift up my bra, open my legs and then told me to squat, to make sure I wasn't bringing in any contrabands into the facility. I felt so violated. Then the nurse told me to step on the scale and it read 125pd. I couldn't believe I had gotten so skinny. Being that I always held a healthy 140pds.

After we entered the unit the girls were looking at me like a piece of meat. When I would take showers the girls would be outside my shower staring at me and I was so scared. I felt sick to my stomach I stayed in bed for a whole week. The room was very small, cold, with twin bunks, a small sink, toilet, and a small TV on the wall with two other cell mates.

I started attending church and bible study groups in jail. One day in church the minister said "sometimes God allow certain things to happen in your life to get your attention, like hello remember me." Right then I felt something all through my body and I knew that message was for me. I was living the fast life and making all this money but I wasn't going to church or praying the way I knew I should. I would always pray over my money and say quick prayers in my heart but that was all I had time for. So God had to snatch me out of my environment, away from work and away from Jake so he could get me alone.

Once I realized what was happening, I immediately began praying, asking god to forgive me. I started meditating on Psalm 143 day and night.

1. Lord, hear my prayer,
   listen to my cry for mercy;
   in your faithfulness and righteousness
   come to my relief.

2. Do not bring your servant into judgment,
   for no one living is righteous before you.

3. The enemy pursues me,
   he crushes me to the ground;
   he makes me dwell in the darkness
   like those long dead.

4. So my spirit grows faint within me;
   my heart within me is dismayed.

5. I remember the days of long ago;
   I meditate on all your works

and consider what your hands have done.

6. I spread out my hands to you;
   I thirst for you like a parched land.[a]

7. Answer me quickly, Lord;
   my spirit fails.
   Do not hide your face from me
   or I will be like those who go down to the pit.

8. Let the morning bring me word of your unfailing love,
   for I have put my trust in you.
   Show me the way I should go,
   for to you I entrust my life.

9. Rescue me from my enemies, Lord,
   for I hide myself in you.

10. Teach me to do your will,
    for you are my God;
    may your good Spirit
    lead me on level ground.

11. For your name's sake, Lord, preserve my life;
    in your righteousness, bring me out of trouble.

12. In your unfailing love, silence my enemies;
    destroy all my foes,
    for I am your servant.

As time went on the same women that I was afraid of, started cooking for me, cleaning for me, doing my laundry, braiding my hair, and I even started a workout class for us when we would go outside or to the gym. Most of the women were in jail for drugs prostitution, violence, or scams. But as I got to know them individually, these ladies were very smart funny talented women. They made me feel alive again and we had been clean from drugs. I would eat three times a day and I gained back my weight. Even though I was in jail I was in a much healthier environment.

After my workout with the ladies one afternoon, one of the inmates approached me and said Jake said he's here and that he had gotten arrested for fighting someone after a party. The next day Jake and I were in court together, handcuffed hands and feet in separate holding cells. I was so shock that Jake had gotten arrested but it felt so good to have him near. I hadn't seen him in so long except for the few times he came to court on my behave-asking the judge to release me. I was denied bail twice before by the same judge even though I didn't have a record and it was my first offense.

When they called Jake and I out to be seen by the judge I notice my mother, my aunt, both of my uncles, my cousins, and my grandmother and my older sister Keisha from the Virgin Islands was on one side of the room and Jake's family was on the other. The judge told me the only reason he kept me in jail for two months was to teach me a lesson. He dropped all charges against me and I got released. I fell to my knees and praised God for his mercy. As for Jake... well the judge revoked his bail and later giving over a six year sentence.

Chapter 5

Betrayal

I went back home to live with Tina and Clifford even though it felt uncomfortable to be back in my room after having my own place. I continued working at the club and I had to pay my aunt $600 a month for a room that was cold with no TV. and I barely used. I would also give my aunt $20 for offering at church. The whole church started talking about me when they found out I was a dancer and I had been in jail. So I stop attending.

On my way to work one day I was running late and I got into a cab. He was this handsome man name Luca. I notice he had some rosary chains hanging from his rea-view mirror and a small black bible in the corner of his dashboard. I could see him looking at me so I smiled. He asked me if I was ok and I said yes. Then I ask if he was a man of God and he replied "oh yes I am, I am your angel sent from God." From then on Luca became my personal driver and good friends.

Luca was like the father I never had. Whenever I needed someone to talk to he would listen and he always made me laugh. Luca always told me to pray to God and he would take me to his church. Whenever I needed help Luca was always there for me and he even taught me how to drive. I got my license at the age of 21 and I bought my first car fresh off the lot. It was a 2006 Honda Accord Coupe name Princess. Then I moved out of my aunt's house and moved into my own studio apartment.

I would visit Jake once or twice a week in jail and prison. He was only 30 minutes away but it would take me the whole day when I went to visit him between the buses trains, commuter rail and sometimes a cab. Then I would have to wait another 30-45 minutes to see him because the prison would be packed with family and friends so they would let a certain amount of visitors in at a time. I would put money on the phone so we could talk and commissary in his account every week or when needed. We would write each other and I made sure he had his pictures. On his birthday I was outside if his cell widow, holding signs of I love and miss you, balloons and a bottle of Moet. I popped it open, poured it out for Jake, and then blew him a kiss. All the guys were looking out the windows and they started banging so hard on the windows.

After a year of holding Jake down faithfully, I found out Jake had slept with or had sexual relations with all my co-workers even Peaches and Candy. He had these women talking about me and smiling in my face the whole time. I felt so betrayed and I called off the engagement.

I reached back out to my former boyfriend Jesse from high school. He was my first love and my first everything. We had broken up in high school because I had moved back to Florida after me and Clifford got into a physical altercation when I was 17. But I returned to finish school. Jesse and I started hanging out again and I became pregnant. Something Jesse and I always wanted back in high school. I was afraid to break the new so Jake because I would still keep in touch with him and send him money whenever I could. But he told me if I had an abortion he would try to forgive me. I refused and continued my pregnancy.

Jesse had an anger management problem ever since high school and he had gotten kicked out of his house for fighting with his dad Dylan. I welcomed him into my home and he was working only part-time so I continued working up until I was six months pregnant to keep up with the bills. When I was seven months pregnant we travel to Florida. My mother and my sister Alexa had thrown us a beautiful baby shower and all my family and friends were there.

When Jesse and I returned to Boston, as I was lying on the bed alone, I saw myself arriving at Jesse's house and I was standing outside my car with my baby. My baby looked at least six or seven years of age. Then I saw Olivia sitting down in the kitchen with her Daughter. I didn't know what that meant so I prayed on it and I brushed it off.

When my water broke at 5am, Jesse rushed me to the hospital. After many dosage of the epidural, it still was not strong enough. I was in labor for 20 hours and I was in excruciating pain. By the time the doctor decided to give me a higher dosage of the epidural, I gave birth to a healthy baby boy name King. When the nurse placed him in my arms, his eyes were open and he was smiling. I thanked God for the blessing he had given me. Olivia and Dylan allowed Jesse and me to move in with them, until we were able to get back on our feet. I had to put my furniture in storage and I had to put my car up until I resumed back to work.

After the birth of our son though, Jesse and I started arguing over his infidelities or him not trusting me because of my recent profession. When he was angry he would become very destructive at times. He would break the windows in the house, he would break my TVs, my lap tops, and he would even vandalize my car.one night when king was 8 months old, I was rocking him to sleep. Jesse had said something rude to me and I replied the same way. He jumped on me from the back and began punching me, trying to pull King out of my hand. Olivia, Dylan, his baby brother and his grandmother had to pull him off of me. I was admitted into the hospital with a black eye and King was ok. The hospital notified Department of Children and Families (DCF) and I couldn't return to Olivia's house with my son or else they would have taken King from me. So I admitted king and I into a homeless shelter and Jesse was arrested.

I enrolled back into school at Everest Institute. I became an ambassador of my class and I graduated with honors. I was hired on my internship at a diabetic clinic as a Medical Administrator. After Jesse had served 8months for the assault, I would allow him to see King every other weekend and on holidays. But when Jesse would watch king while I was working, he would call my job over a hundred times, checking to see if I was at work. He would rush me to pick up king and one night after work, we got into a disagreement and he slammed my car door so hard the air bags hit me so hard in my chest. I could barely breathe and king was in the back seat. Jesse went into his house, grabbed his bag and left us there. I ended all contact with Jesse from then on.

Chapter 6

Abandonment

King and I would have to take the bus in the snow and the rain. We had a 9 o'clock curfew at the shelter and the busses would stop running at 6pm. If you were late, after the third time, they would terminate your stay. You had to provide your own food and no men were allowed. We would also have to do job and housing search during the day with our workers that were assigned to each of us. I couldn't believe I went from having my own place and my own car to now being homeless in a shelter with my son. It felt like God had pulled the rug from beneath me.

After two years of moving from shelter to shelter with my son, I finally had my own place again and I had saved up enough money to get my car running. Things at work were going well and I went above and beyond for the patients. But even though things started to look up for king and I, I still had this pain in my chest for king. I grew up without my father and I never wanted him to go through that.

One Halloween day Luca had brought me to the grocery store and as I was shopping, I made eye contact this guy name Seth. He was very good-looking, athletic body, with light brown eyes, and freshly done dreads, with 8 packed abs. I immediately looked away and continued shopping. I looked back and I saw Seth peeking in the corner down the aisle so I smiled and kept on walking. As I was standing in the checkout line, Seth approached me; we began talking and exchanged numbers.

Seth was a flyboy and he was always about making money. He was very funny, outgoing, and everyone loved him. After 8 months of getting to know one another we got engaged and I introduced him to King. Seth would tell me to kick my feet up and relax, while he gave King Baths, changed his diapers, tucked him in at night and he would take King to and from school. Seth would even cook and clean for us. I told god I had to have him and I knew he was my husband.

That same year I became pregnant with my second son Prince Jr. King was so excited to be an older brother. But when I was four months pregnant Seth told me that he lied to me about his name and age. He was five years younger than me not one. So when I was 22 he was 17. I couldn't believe he hid this from me and I was so enraged with him. But I was already in love with him so I forgave him.

When Seth introduced king and I to his family his mother Cynthia said she knew who King was and that King was her nephew son Jesse. When Jesse found out I was dating his cousin and I was with child, he started calling me and making threats. He told me if I don't end the relationship with Seth he would harm King and I. I was already deep into the relationship with Seth, so we decided to continue with our relationship and Jesse was furious. He started to deny King was his son and he even went on Facebook and told the world King was not his son.

My heart was so broken. It felt like a big whole in my chest. I couldn't understand how someone I once loved, the person I bared a child for, could turn against us this way. Never did I ever think Jesse would be the one to walk out of his son's life. I knew for sure if I ever had kids it would have been from him. Olivia agreed with Jesse that "she doesn't know me anymore and that she's was done with me". A time that was supposed to be filled with joy, once again had turned into rain.

During my pregnancy I became very depressed and I would have many mood swings. This was Seth first child so the whole pregnancy thing was new for him. My once sweet loving charmer had started to change. We would argue often and he would say things like "I'm just using the baby as an excuse or I didn't know pregnancy would be this hard."

When I was eight months pregnant after Seth had finish giving me a bubble bath one night while king was asleep, we had a disagreement. He called me out of my name and I said your mother. Seth pulled me by my hair up and down the stairs, took a scissors cut my hair and then sat on top of my stomach fighting me, until I was able to get away and get help. I was transported to the hospital by the EMS. Prince and I were ok but Cynthia was furious with me and told Seth if I loved him I would not have gotten him arrested. Not once did she call to see if I or prince was ok. She never liked me nor did Olivia or Jakes mom. I have always been respectable and kind to these women even though I knew they did not care for me.

While Seth was in jail I would call out of work often because at times it would be difficult finding a babysitter five days a week. The boss did not understand and according to her words "she still has a clinic to run. After the third warning I was laid off and I started receiving government assistance."

A few weeks before my due date, Seth came home and I decided to stay in the relationship. We both agreed to attend couple counseling for the sake of our children. Seth is all king knew as a father and I did not want to bring another man into our home, nor did I want to bare another man's child. Yes I was ashamed and embarrassed but I just wasn't ready to be a single mother raising two kids. I never saw that for my life and I always knew I was going to be happily married with kids.

Cynthia and Seth sister Candice had thrown us a baby shower and our kids had more than enough clothes and shoes. Cynthia and Candice always loved shopping for the kids, especially for their birthdays and holidays. Cynthia had this delicious marble cake made and Seth and I had our beautiful king and queen chairs set up by Candice. Seth and I were dressed in the same color orange as well as King. And there were plenty food drinks and laughter.

The day of my delivery I went into labor at 9am and I allowed Candice to be present for the birth since Seth had made her the godmother of prince. After six hours of labor prince shoulder got stuck and he could not breathe. I started to pray and by the time the nurses finally got him out he was purple and blue and Seth was not allowed to cut the cord They cleaned prince off, suctioned his nose and mouth, as well as some reflex testing, and I heard my baby's cry. My heart was filled with joy and I thanked God. The nurse then laid prince on my chest and we began bonding. Seth and Candice held him after.

When prince was two months old Seth and I had stooped at his parents' house. And Seth father Sean greeted us with lots of love and affection. When Cynthia and Candice saw us, they immediately began yelling and screaming at me saying "take your child and go!" Candice took prince from Sean and gave him to Cynthia and Cynthia gave prince back to me. I couldn't believe prince own grandmother and his auntie who watched him born, were passing prince around telling us to leave. I was in shock and I couldn't even move. Candice then threw prince baby bag at my car and yelled "take your child and go!" Cynthia agreed with her daughter, handed me back the rest of prince belonging, and then said "I don't like how u treat my son." Seth was furious and began fighting with Candice. For a whole year Cynthia and Candice was not allowed to see the kids until after prince first birthday when they had finally decided to apologize for what they had done.

Chapter 7

yr 2 cycle of violence

Seth and I were still very hurt by what his family had done but things started to look up for us. Seth had finally gotten his license and he was so excited. He enrolled back into school for construction and he graduated with honors as well as completing anger management and fatherhood class. We started fasting for our relationship and we would even visit different churches with our kids. Seth even gave his life to Christ. We started spending more time as a family and I became pregnant with our third child. But one afternoon when king was three years old, Seth had left to pick him up while I relaxed with prince. An hour or so later Seth came rushing through the doors with King in his hand. King had glass in his hair and he was bleeding. Life became unreal and I heard my ears popping. I could barely scream and I asked what happened to my son?

Seth had run into Jesse after picking King up from school and they got into an altercation. Jesse then walked over to the side where king was sitting and punched the window so hard the glass broke and it hit king in the face and head. We immediately took king to the hospital and he was treated for minor injuries. Jesse was given a year sentence for hurting his own son.

During my pregnancy with my third child Seth and I was preparing our boys for a new member to the family. The boys would help us decorate the baby's room and they would even feel the baby's kicks. King was turning four and prince had just turned one. Prince was still crawling but he was learning how to walk. But when I was 8 months pregnant on mother's day as well as king birthday, Seth and I had been up all night the day before preparing for king's birthday. I was feeling a little agitated and tired. After kings party on our way home I was annoyed that Seth wasn't being understanding towards my feelings and we started arguing.

Seth told me I wasn't his type and that he was only settling for our kids. I got really angry and we started fighting on the highway with our boys sleeping in the back seat. I tried to jump out of the car so I could get away from him and a few people that were driving by saw the altercation, called the police. Moments later we were pulled over. Seth shirt was ripped as well as my dress, and my hair was pulled out. Seth was arrested and our boys were taken by the department of children and families (DCF) that following Monday, after my case had just been closed from the incident with Jesse.

During court the judge wanted to take my unborn child as well but my aunt and uncle agreed to take my kids so the judge gave them temporary custody of my kids. The judge and the lawyers were so rude to Seth and I. the judge wouldn't even allow us to speak to him only through our lawyers. But our lawyers barely listened to anything we had to say. My lawyer even told me one time "you're just like any other Domestic Violence victim that comes in here." Then she pointed to a line with 20-30 women with kids waiting to be seen and told me to go sit with them.

DCF even contacted Olivia and Jesse and they were there asking the judge for a paternity test so they could make sure that Jesse was king's father. I couldn't believe what was happening but the judge denied there request and said "if he's not your son that's just another child without a father."

The judge then sentenced Seth to a year in jail and I had to complete a Domestic Violence program (DV) to regain custody of my boys.

It was very hard for me to attend the DV groups because I couldn't understand why I was there. I felt like I took good care of my kids and I am very over protective of my kids. My kids had more than enough food, clothes, shoes toys and they never went without. It would break my heart to hear those women stories about being abuse or being the abuser. Women would come to group right after a visit with their kids and they would be distraught. DCF had taken their kids also and if you got approved for visitation, it would be once a week for one or two hours and sometimes supervised. If you didn't have anyone qualified to take your kids for you, then DCF would put them with a stranger and you would not know where or who your child is with. I couldn't imagine going through this with my boys.

After two or three cycles of taking the DV groups I finally understood what I was doing to my kids. Even though I wasn't physically abusing them, I was mentally abusing my kids. I gained so much knowledge on the warning signs of DV before and after; I learned the different forms of abuse physically mentally and emotionally. When I was growing up I would see men come and go and I never wanted that for my kids so I was trying to keep our family together.

Chapter 8

Yr 3 bittersweet

The following month Kayla threw me beautiful baby shower and I gave birth to a healthy baby girl name princess without Seth. Prince finally started walking. And this was a very stressful time for me but when I held my princess in my arms, all I felt was joy and love. She was so beautiful with a head full of hair. Princess had this big smile on her face with these cute little dimples like her daddy. Tina, Clifford, Kayla, Luca, my grandmother, King, Prince and even Cynthia and Candice was there to welcomed princess.

I wasn't allowed to visit Seth due to the situation but I would always send him pictures of his princess as well as his boys. I would put commissary in his account and money on the phone so he could talk to his kids. I finally gained custody of my boys back and I enrolled back into college. I got my certificate in Early Childhood Education and I would volunteer three times a week at a head start as a teacher assistant. I learned a lot about children wellbeing, thinking abilities, health, as well as their social and emotional development.

Seth came home when princess was 10 months old and he had just missed prince 2nd birthday. Princess fell in love with her daddy and everything was about princess. On her first birthday she had three parties. Princess was dress in her beautiful princess dress with her matching crown on her head. I was so grateful Seth was home in time for her birthday.

The following morning around 1am I had awakened from a terrible dream. I was driving my car and I stared looking for something underneath my seat, when suddenly I crashed. Prince and princess were in the back seat but I couldn't see Seth or King. Princess was on top of prince and they both were crying. I notice princess was still a baby and prince was a teenager with a big cut on the side of his head. I immediately began praying over Seth and I as well as our kids. And then I put oil on our heads.

Chapter 9

Grace

I was at the gym running 3.6mph on the treadmill when I slipped and busted my head open. I tried to stop the blood that was coming out but it was too much. People started coming over asking me if I was ok and as I went to lift up my head I was walking down this long bright cold hallway and I knocked on this door. Cynthia opened the door and I saw Seth family sitting down at these tables. So I walked inside and I sat down at a table as well. Everyone was staring at me and it felt like they did not want me there. Seth awakened me out of my dream and I told him what I had dreamt. He reassured me everything was ok and that I had been over working myself with the gym, school our kids and stress.

For Fourth of July Seth and I decided to take a road trip to Florida with our kids to visit my family. We packed our cooler with plenty food and drinks and our kids all had their tablets. We rented a 2016 Chrysler 200 but at the last minute, as we were getting ready to hit the road, I notice all the seatbelts in the back seat were broken. So I had to use the straps on top of the car seat with the hooks and fasten them into the top of the seats. I never really used these hooks. I usually just buckle car seats in with the seatbelts and then fasten kids in with the buckles in their car seats.

We made a few bathroom stops on the way but Seth drove straight with no sleep.at 715am in south Carolina I had awaken from a nap and we were still on the highway driving so fast. I looked over at Seth and he was going in and out of sleep. I panic and I screamed his name. He immediately opened his eyes and turned the wheel. We ended up on the side of the road sliding of fast on the bumps. Seth tried to stop the car but it would not stop. We flew off the road and I quickly took my arms and blocked the opening so none of the kids would fly to the front. We hit an embankment and bounced back unto the road. All the airbags came out and it hit me in my chest I could barely breathe or talk. I remembered seeing a black hawk in the sky crowing. I looked over to Seth and his face was badly hurt. I was so afraid to look in the backseat I started crying asking Seth are the kids ok. The car was totaled and I was admitted into the hospital with a fractured spine and Seth had minor injuries. As for our kid, they were untouched by the grace of God!

I was released that same night from the hospital and we checked into a hotel. We were unable to rent another car and all the busses and cab were miles away. We had to pay over a hundred dollars just to get a cab. We were running low on cash so my mother had to send us money to take the train back to Boston. We were stuck in South Carolina for three days and on our way back to Boston we were kicked off the train in North Carolina for arguing. We had no money and stranded with our three kids. Later that night North Carolina police department and the department of children and families paid our hotel for the night and paid our trip back to Boston. I stayed quite the whole way back and it felt like longest trip in hell.

When we finally arrived I was still in tremendous pain. The following day I had just gotten back from my doctor's appointment and Seth was dressed with his bag packed. He said he had just spoken with his older brother Pete about what happened on our trip and he decided to leave with him. I was on perkasets and I really needed his help with the kids. So I tried to stop him from leaving but he would not listen to anything I had to say. The time that I needed him the most I couldn't believe that this was the time he chose to leave.

Almost a week later Seth stopped by to see his kids, and he was apologized for leaving. He told me he only had only20 dollars in his pocket and nowhere to go. But as I was looking through his phone I saw a message from Seth asking for his former girlfriend's number, dated the same day he walked out on me and his kids. I was enraged and right then the devil took ahold of us both. I began hitting him and I called him all the names in the book. Seth grabbed me by my neck and said "you're going to die today." He then began choking me and I was kicking and punching him but he would not let go of my neck. I remember going in and out of consciousness and I felt like I was going to die. Finally he said "say sorry!" I was so scared I said sorry and he let go of my neck. He apologized for what he had done then ask if we could get through this. I was still terrified I lied and said yes. But I knew I had to make the hardest decision of my life because if I stayed with Seth he would either kill me or my kids would be taken away so I chose my children.

Chapter 10

Yr 4 Halloween

I was driving so fast side to side trying to get away. My heart was racing so fast and I didn't say a word. The whole time I was driving someone was next to me saying "I like this nigga, we need this nigga on our team" his voice sound so convincing and after desperately trying to get away and failed, I finally stop the car. I was breathing so hard hoping what this man was saying was true. Then I looked up and I was three or four guys coming towards me. The guy that was talking to me was trying to say something to them. But this black skinny, kin of tall, guy lifted his right eye his hoodie and cocked his hand back and hit me so hard in my head. I awaken frighten out of my dream breathing so hard. And I remember thanking God it was just a dream.

I started taking walks in the park and I would meditate for hours. I would ask God what is my purpose and where am I going. I remember even feeling angry towards god for allowing this to happen to me and I would wear chokers around my neck to symbolize the attack. I was still worried about Seth being on the streets with nowhere to go. So I would always pray god keep him safe and help him be a better man for his kids.

I reconnected with Sasha from the grizzles and she had just gotten back to Boston. She had left to Florida after college to peruse directing and came back to finish her latest music video. She stared me in it as her model and the video was about this lady doing voodoo on me. In the one of the scene Sasha handed me a black rose and I was murdered.

I started working at a bikini bar and I would pay Sasha to babysit for me. I would work five days a week from7pm-2am. Seth would still try to come back home but I was determined to let him go. It was killing me to leave him out there because Seth would go from house to house car to car, and even a shelter. But I had given him almost four years of my life and things were getting worse.

That Thursdays morning the kids weren't feeling well so they all stayed home from school. I allowed Seth to come by and he dropped off some diapers and medicine for the kids. He was rushing so he could get the back bumper on his car fix but as he was leaving he asked the kids what Halloween costumes they wanted and left. Halloween was two weeks away and the kids were anxious.

The next day Seth took king and princess to school and I took prince to his doctor appointment. Later that night Sasha came over as usual to babysit while I went to work. The next day I woke up with this bad feeling all through my body. The kids had left with their grandparents to buy their pumpkins for Halloween and I was nervous. I had those feeling before and it was never good.

Later that night I was on my way to work when Seth started call and texting me. He wanted to know how me and his kids were doing but I didn't reply. I had a few drinks at work so I left work early around 12am. There was no parking in front of my house so I had to park a block away. I took a shower ate a pizza kiss my kids goodnight and passed out after 2am Sunday morning.

I awakened out of my sleep around 6am that morning and I was so angry. Ladies! You know the feeling when you have a dream about your man cheating on you? Well I had a dream Seth had an affair with someone I knew. I immediately grabbed my phone to call him when I notice three text messages from him after3am. He was looking for me and he didn't see my car at work or in front of the house. I text him back and waited for him to call me back so I could ask him about my dream.

Around 1pm I notice Seth still didn't text me back so I started doing the kids hair for school the next day. As I was finishing up king's hair Seth homeboy Doe texted me say "sorry for your loss" as I was texting Doe back to ask him what he was talking about. My other homeboy Dread called me and said "Seth was shot and killed early this morning." I immediately remembered my dreams and my whole world stopped! I was in such disbelief and I fell to my knees weeping all night.

The next day Pete came over to tell me the news. He took us to see Cynthia and she blamed me for what had happened to her son. Even though I was extremely hurt I still gave her my last thousand dollars to help in any way. I had never really experience something so tragic except for when I lost my grandfather to cancer when I was 16. But just when I though it couldn't get any worse, here I was a widow at 28 with three kids.

At the funeral it was packed with lots of family and friends and Olivia and Jesse was even there. Olivia came over and said hello to king and I but Jesse acted like he didn't see us. During the service I couldn't help but notice there were no pictures being shown of Seth and his kids just him and his family. Then inside the obituary right in the center was this big picture of Seth and Jesse. It stated king was Seth step son and it mentioned nothing about me, nor was I mentioned the service. Seth family was one side comforting one another and me and my kids was alone with no one helping me. Not once did they ask if I was ok or did I need any help. My aunt and uncle had offered to accompany me to the funeral but I was sure my kids and I would be ok.

On the way to the burial I remember feeling confused and angry inside. I couldn't believe that all of this was happening and that we were in a limo following a Herse, with Seth in it to be buried. I kept asking god how is this happening? Is this really real? When we arrived I could see some people were already there and some were getting out of their cars. The limo driver allowed everyone to step out except me. Then seconds later the funeral coordinator opened my door took my hand and he excused everyone out of the way. Right then a path opened up and he escorted me to the front where Sean and my kids were standing. The sun came out and shined so bright on me the whole time the coordinator was speaking.

Everyone then threw their flowers in and said their goodbyes as well as our kids. It started to rain and I began to weep, asking God why? I trusted you with his life lord. Why? When I let him go I didn't mean for you to let go too. Why lord? I don't understand what's happening you are a good God. Where were you and your angels? Is this what I get for choosing my kids? I thought I was doing the right thing lord. You must have thought about my kids before you allowed this to happen. Why lord? Why? I surrender I give myself to you. What do you want from me?

End of book

Seth came walking through the front door and the kids ran to him screaming Daddy! Daddy! I said no!

Seth came walking through the front door the kids ran to him and yelled Daddy! Daddy! I said no!

Seth came walking through the front door again and the kids ran to him Yelling Daddy! Daddy!

The next day I was in church praying and I could see Seth in the casket dressed in all white with his eyes closed. A loud trumpet went off and he opened his eyes. I felt something cold behind me so I turned around and it was Seth. I began yelling and screaming he's alive he lives thank you Jesus glory to your name. Then I awaken out my dream with this strong painless feeling in my heart

Printed in the United States
by Baker & Taylor Publisher Services